Manifestation Journal for Black Women

Powerful Law of Attraction Guided Journal and Exercises to Attract Wealth, Abundance, Love, and Happiness

Layla Moon

Table of Contents

4 FREE Gifts

To help you along your spiritual journey, I've created 4 FREE bonus eBooks.

You can get instant access by signing up to my email newsletter below.

On top of the 4 free books, you will also receive weekly tips along with free book giveaways, discounts, and so much more.

All of these bonuses are 100% free with no strings attached. You don't need to provide any personal information except your email address.

To get your bonus, go to:

https://dreamlifepress.com/four-free-gifts

Spirit Guides for Beginners: How to Hear the Universe's Call and Communicate with Your Spirit Guide and Guardian Angels

Guided by Moon herself, inspired by her own experiences and knowledge that has been passed down by hundreds of generations for thousands of years, you'll discover everything you need to know to;

- Understanding what the call of the universe is

- How to hear and comprehend it

- Knowing who and what your spirit guides and guardian angels are

- Learning how to connect, start a conversation, and listen to your guides

- How to manifest your dreams with the help of the cosmic source

- Learning how to start living the life you want to live

- And so much more…

Law of Attraction: Manifest Your Desire

Learn how to tap into the infinite power of the universe and manifest everything you want in life.

Includes:

- Law of Attraction: Manifest Your Desire ebook

- Law of Attraction Workbook

- Cheat sheets and checklists so make sure you're on the right path

Hoodoo Book of Spells for Beginners: Easy and effective Rootwork, Conjuring, and Protection Spells for Healing and Prosperity

Harness the power of one of the greatest magics. Hoodoo is a powerful force ideal for holding negativity at bay, promoting positivity in all areas in your life, offering protection to the things you love, and ultimately taking control of your destiny.

Inside, you will discover:

- How to get started with Hoodoo in your day-to-day life

- How to use conjuration spells to manifest the life you want to live

- How casting protection spells can help you withstand the toughest of times

- Break cycles of bad luck and promote good fortune throughout your life

- Hoodoo to encourage prosperity and financial stability

- How to heal using Hoodoo magic, both short-term and long-term traumas and troubles

- Remove curses and banish pain, suffering, and negativity from your life

- And so much more…

Book of Shadows

A printable PDF to support you in your spiritual transformation.

Within the pages, you will find:

- Potion and tinctures tracking sheet

- Essential oils log pages

- Herbs log pages

- Magical rituals and spiritual body goals checklist

- Tarot reading spread sheets

- Weekly moon and planetary cycle tracker

- And so much more

Get all the resources for FREE by visiting the link below

https://dreamlifepress.com/four-free-gifts

"Every great dream begins with a dreamer. Always remember, you have within you the strength, the patience, and the passion to reach for the stars to change the world."

- Harriet Tubman

"What you think you become.
What you feel you attract.
What you imagine you create."

- Buddha

How You Got This Way

"Once you make a decision, the universe conspires to make it happen."
- Ralph Waldo Emerson

I used to believe that quotes like these were ridiculous. I, too, was bemused. What the hell were they on about? I mean, it's not like I cared. I am a black woman. Did black women really believe these things? And besides, what little I knew about self-help was unforgivably cheesy: it smelled of desperation.

At the same time, I had a long list of things I wanted to change about my life. And as I look back, I realize how desperately I needed help and how little I was doing to help myself. I mean, even though I was alive and well, I had had to deal with a wide range of problems my entire life. My life was in disarray. But, in comparison to what I knew I was capable of, I was, to put it mildly, very unimpressed.

I always thought:

"Come on, is this the best I can do?"

"Really? I'm only going to slug through life and accept what I think I can get? Day in, day out? Again and again?"

"And do I intend to spend another year dating weirdos just so I can be in all these shaky, noncommittal relationships and cause even more drama? Really?"

"The most common way people give up their power is by thinking they don't have any."

- Alice Walker

The best decision I ever made was to stop accepting things as they were. I chose to tap into the black woman's power. I chose to stand up and stand tall. I wrote this book to provide black women with the critical information that is frequently lacking but necessary for successful manifestation using the Law of Attraction.

Sisters, I need you to know that your reality will shift as you recognize the role and power of the Law of Attraction because you will realize how powerful you are. You'll begin to recognize your thoughts as energy: energy that can be focused, clarified, and shaped into things, experiences, and events.

Being a black woman doesn't stop you from achieving anything! If you want happiness and fulfillment in your life, you can choose to manifest what you want in relationships, bank account, job, health, or other areas. It takes effort to make your fairytale a reality. And that's fine. You can start doing that now. There's so much more to gain if you take a risk on yourself and try something new.

However, the Law of Attraction is not just another feel-good exercise to help you improve your life or circumstances. Instead, it will transform you if you work with it. As your circumstances improve and you begin to use your intrinsic ability to manifest, you will experience some kind of transformation - manifesting what you want in life as you learn to play with this power.

Working with the Law of Attraction can lead to a deeper connection with your spirit and the laws of the Universe. This book will take you on a journey to discover the incredible power you have within you to harness the Law of Attraction for a happier, healthier, and more fulfilled life.

Sisters, in this journal, you will learn how to achieve your goals while having fun, how to fill your heart with the form of love you desire, how to relax in a comfortable life, and how to express your spirit's most genuine, highest calling. By fully engaging in the Law of Attraction, you will discover many of the Universe's secrets within yourself.

This Black Women's Manifestation Journal goes beyond the typical scope of a manifestation journal. It's a proclamation journal where you can write your objectives, visions, obstacles, and resolutions. This journal will help you track where you were and where you are heading. I created this journal to show you how much you can accomplish when you trust the process.

The manifestation techniques outlined in this book will trigger the energy attraction of the object of your desire. They'll take care of initiating the alignment. This book includes principles, exercises, questions, tasks, and tips that will guide you through your journey of manifestation. At the end of each chapter, you will find a task that needs completion before moving to the next page.

Write A Message For Your Future Self

In this section, I want you to write a message for your future self. This message should be a promise to yourself that you will stay committed to this journey of manifestation, that your journey will be fruitful, and that your desires are becoming a reality.

When you have finished reading this entire journal and completed all the exercises, I want you to read this message again so you can see how far you've come and how much progress you've made.

Dear future self

_____
_____
_____
_____
_____
_____
_____
_____
_____
_____
_____
_____
_____
_____
_____
_____
_____
_____
_____
_____
_____
_____
_____
_____

Dear future self

_____

_____

_____

_____

_____

_____

_____

_____

_____

_____

_____

_____

_____

_____

_____

_____

_____

_____

_____

_____

_____

_____

_____

_____

_____

_____

_____

_____

_____

_____

_____

Dear future self

Dear future self

What Doesn't Kill You Only Makes You Stronger

The first step of every personal development journey is to honestly acknowledge what you are struggling with and note them down. In the space provided below, list out the things you struggle with and have issues overcoming.

- _____
- _____
- _____
- _____
- _____
- _____
- _____
- _____
- _____
- _____
- _____
- _____
- _____
- _____
- _____
- _____
- _____
- _____
- _____
- _____
- _____
- _____
- _____
- _____
- _____
- _____
- _____

- _____
- _____
- _____
- _____
- _____
- _____
- _____
- _____
- _____
- _____
- _____
- _____
- _____
- _____
- _____
- _____
- _____
- _____
- _____
- _____
- _____
- _____
- _____
- _____
- _____
- _____
- _____
- _____
- _____
- _____
- _____
- _____

- _____
- _____
- _____
- _____
- _____
- _____
- _____
- _____
- _____
- _____
- _____
- _____
- _____
- _____
- _____
- _____
- _____
- _____
- _____
- _____
- _____
- _____
- _____
- _____
- _____
- _____
- _____
- _____
- _____
- _____
- _____

- _____
- _____
- _____
- _____
- _____
- _____
- _____
- _____
- _____
- _____
- _____
- _____
- _____
- _____
- _____
- _____
- _____
- _____
- _____
- _____
- _____
- _____
- _____
- _____
- _____
- _____
- _____
- _____
- _____
- _____
- _____

- _____
- _____
- _____
- _____
- _____
- _____
- _____
- _____
- _____
- _____
- _____
- _____
- _____
- _____
- _____
- _____
- _____
- _____
- _____
- _____
- _____
- _____
- _____
- _____
- _____
- _____
- _____
- _____
- _____
- _____
- _____
- _____

- _____
- _____
- _____
- _____
- _____
- _____
- _____
- _____
- _____
- _____
- _____
- _____
- _____
- _____
- _____
- _____
- _____
- _____
- _____
- _____
- _____
- _____
- _____
- _____
- _____
- _____
- _____
- _____
- _____
- _____
- _____
- _____

- _____
- _____
- _____
- _____
- _____
- _____
- _____
- _____
- _____
- _____
- _____
- _____
- _____
- _____
- _____
- _____
- _____
- _____
- _____
- _____
- _____
- _____
- _____
- _____
- _____
- _____
- _____
- _____
- _____
- _____
- _____

- _____
- _____
- _____
- _____
- _____
- _____
- _____
- _____
- _____
- _____
- _____
- _____
- _____
- _____
- _____
- _____
- _____
- _____
- _____
- _____
- _____
- _____
- _____
- _____
- _____
- _____
- _____
- _____
- _____
- _____
- _____

CHAPTER ONE

Principles of Self-Care

"My mission in life is not merely to survive, but to thrive; and to do so with some passion, some compassion, some humor, and some style."
- Maya Angelou

People often underestimate how much self-care impacts your manifestation process. I can confidently say that if you are not practicing self-care, you are doing something wrong. When you decide to follow your aspirations, you are stretched and challenged in ways you never expected, and you are shaped into becoming more of who you are at your core. It's easy to lose yourself in the process and do more harm than good, and that's why it's important to remember to look after yourself while chasing your ambitions.

What is self-care? Self-care is a broad word that encompasses everything you intentionally/deliberately do to improve your mental, physical, and emotional health. Unfortunately, self-care is something that many of us overlook. This is why one of the essential terms in its definition is "deliberately." Before you can attain meaningful self-care, you must be aware of your well-being.

It begins with little things like intentionally refusing to do things you are not supposed to. For example, not checking emails late at night because you know it impacts your sleep or significant actions like taking a vacation or scheduling a massage when you need a break instead of pushing yourself. Learning how to nurture yourself is the key to the life you have always wanted. Your mind, body, and soul benefit from effective self-care.

What is the significance of this? Self-care helps you create a positive connection with yourself and others. What you don't have yourself, you can't offer to others. While people mistake self-care for selfishness, this is far from the truth. When you take care of your health, you're not only thinking about your own needs. Instead, you're recharging your batteries to be the greatest version of yourself for others around you. The revitalized energy and excitement you radiate will also help everyone around you.

What Self-Care isn't

Here are some common misunderstandings about self-care and its underlying truths.

1. "Self-care has to be earned."

Self-care is not earned through hard effort or service to others. Self-care can be a pleasure and a need after a long period of hard labor. You are deserving of self-care because you are alive. You are a human being deserving of compassion, love, and kindness from others and yourself. Self-care is a natural right that does not need to be earned.

2. "Self-care is for people who have nothing else to do."

Self-care is necessary for everyone. You may believe that you do not need to care for yourself since you always care for others, but this is not the case. When you take care of yourself, you go on a healing path. Self-care includes your thinking, attitude, and self-talk. Additionally, self-care encompasses the problematic aspects of life, such as saying no, establishing boundaries, and responding to one's emotions. For example, self-care may involve just being kinder to yourself when you make a mistake, releasing yourself from the pressure to perform flawlessly, or speaking to yourself in an encouraging rather than critical tone when you're having a poor day (or a good day). But, of course, self-care is not always pleasurable.

Self-care is a conscious decision to do what is best for you.

3. "Self-care is time-consuming."

No, self-care should not be reduced to being "time-consuming." Self-care does not have to be time-consuming. It is an integral part of human existence, so you have to learn to make time for it. Most people agree that one of the most significant impediments to self-care is lack of time. What you may not realize is that small and quick acts of kindness toward oneself can accumulate to cause beneficial transformation.

Certain self-care activities require little time, such as being less critical of oneself after a mistake, saying no, or taking a deep breath. Additionally, keep in mind that when you're busy and don't have time for self-care, that's when it's most necessary. Being busy and lacking time for self-care is a motivation to prioritize it, not an excuse to disregard it.

Rather than pretending you can't have or don't deserve something, you should figure out precisely what makes you joyful and most alive and then go out and grab it. Good news: you only need to take one essential step to do this. Instead of just desiring/wanting to alter your life, you must decide to do it. "Wanting" is passive. "Deciding," on the other hand, entails doing everything it takes to pursue your goals with the ferocity of a thousand bulls.

There is no need to wait until you reach rock bottom to begin crawling out of the hole. There is nothing more you need to do except decide. And you can do it now. Greatness awaits you.

Principles Of Self-Care That Will Contribute To Your Journey Of Manifestation

#Principle 1

Be nice to yourself and others. The way we communicate to ourselves is crucial to our overall well-being. The words we use to describe ourselves and our thoughts about ourselves have a great deal of influence. A person's behavior, thoughts, and relationships are directly affected by their words. Words have power; use them carefully.

#Principle 2

Be true to yourself. Don't let anyone or thing distract you from being loyal to who you are and what you believe in. Protect yourself from adopting opinions that don't match your life or go against your values.

#Principle 3

Get rid of things that don't belong to you and focus on what does. The time has come to let go of people, things, ideas, and beliefs that no longer serve you. Decide to let go of anything that prevents you from moving on to a higher level of life.

#Principle 4

Listen to, and believe in your inner voice. Create frequent periods of stillness and listen to your soul's desires. The significance of listening to your inner voice is undeniable. For example, when you have a positive mindset and your inner voice is telling you to believe in your capabilities or to trust that what is yours will come to you, trust it to tell you the next move. By paying attention to your inner voice, you are setting your mindset and desires in sync.

#Principle 5

Be flexible and receptive to life's surprises. Allow yourself to be more accepting of what is. Pay attention to your life's cues and proceed on the path it points you toward. It's important to see your experiences as chances for personal development regardless of how positive or negative they may be.

#Principle 6

Align your inner and outside lives. Your words, actions, beliefs, and feelings must all be in sync.

#Principle 7

Attend to your own needs first. Make yourself a priority. Continually show yourself love, care, and compassion. The way you treat yourself sets a strong example of how others should treat you.

#Principle 8

Own your emotions. Feel all your emotions. Sit down with them. Look at them, reflect, introspect, and then let them go in a good way. Resist the temptation to dull your senses with meaningless and harmful routines or habits. Don't be afraid to admit that you're feeling down and find things that will help you feel better.

#Principle 9

Treat your body with respect. Gratitude is an attitude of appreciation for the amazing things your body is capable of. Avoid negative self-talk and falling into the comparison trap. Take care of your body by eating well, getting enough sleep, and exercising. Taking care of your body is like taking care of a sacred temple.

#Principle 10

Make yourself comfortable in the places you're in. Be confident in who you are, no matter what. No one, not even yourself, should dull your brightness.

DAILY AFFIRMATIONS

When it comes to self-care, affirmations are a great way to start off your day. There's evidence suggesting that your thoughts have a greater influence on your behavior than your physical actions. As a person who has battled anxiety, I can attest to this. Morning affirmations are a great way to combat negativity, both internally and externally.

READ THESE OUT LOUD

I intend to savor every second of every moment.

I am tenacious.

I am smart.

I pick my own path to happiness.

I have the knowledge and skills to accomplish anything I set my mind to.

Regardless of the circumstances, I will use positive language and think positive thoughts.

I attract success.

Everything I desire is everything I am entitled to.

Discipline allows me to be at peace.

Every day, I strive to become a better version of myself.

Self-Care Action Plan

In the diagram provided below, create a self-care action plan. In the spaces of each section of the cartwheel, fill in activities you want to start practicing daily. Observe the less-than-impressive aspects of your life and consider what ideas/beliefs may have influenced them. The first step is to know the areas in your life that you know are suffering neglect. When you have a vague idea of this, the next step is to decide on how you can fix it. To achieve success in this area of your life, you need to be intentional about how you go about creating your self-care action plan.

In the center of the cartwheel, using a few words, write words that capture what you want to achieve at the end of this exercise. For example, peace, happiness, free time, fitness, etc.

In the next layer, which is divided into five categories, write out the five categories of your life where you want to be more intentional about practicing self-care.

In the final layer, write out the activities under each category that you want to start practicing.

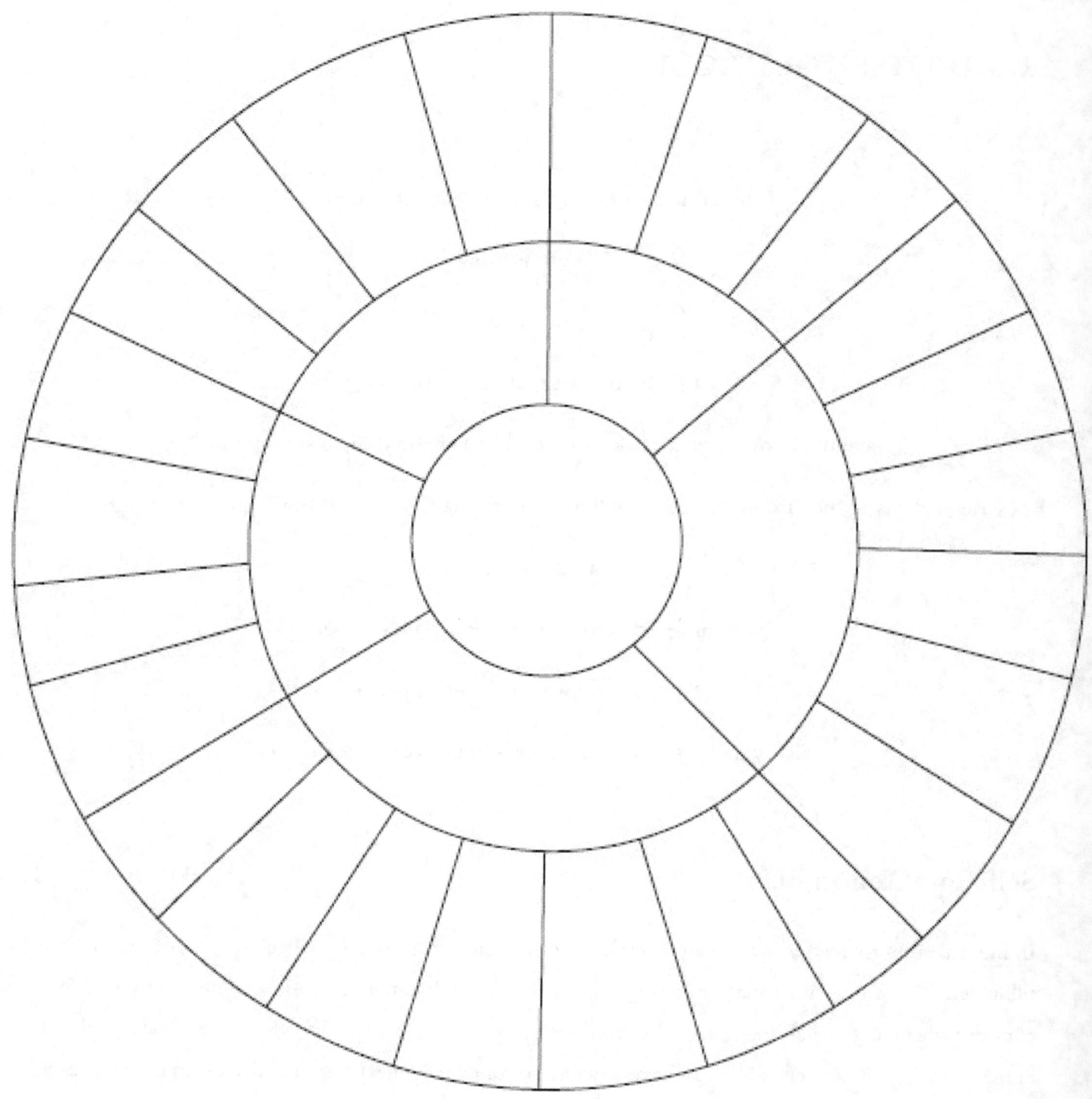

The 30-Day Self-Care Challenge

The 30-day Self-Care Challenge was designed to help you take your self-care more seriously. Every single day for 30 days, write in each square an activity you did that captures the concept of self-care. For example, in the first box, if at the end of that day you were able to go to a spa or you spent the night out with friends, write it in the space provided for that day. At the end of the month, you will see how this challenge will help you take up the habit of practicing self-care.

30 DAY
Self-care Challenge

30 DAY
Self-care Challenge

30 DAY
Self-care Challenge

CHAPTER TWO

The Power of Manifesting and The Law of Attraction

Things That Motivate Me

In this section, I want you to write out what motivates you in life. Why do you desire a good life? Why do you practice self-care? Why do you practice manifesting? Why do you desire an amazing partner? These are a few questions you should ask yourself while you write out the things that motivate you to keep striving, keep being strong, and work towards the life you know you deserve. For example, you could write that you practice self-care daily because you are an amazing person that deserves all the care in the world. With this awesome exercise, you'll be inspired to channel your inner queen warrior. Write out what motivates you below. You are strong, self-assured, and courageous!

Things that motivate me

Things that motivate me

Things that motivate me

"Thoughts become things. If you see it in your mind, you'll hold it in your hand."

- Bob Proctor

What if you could have anything you desired simply by thinking about it?

Wouldn't it be great if you could effortlessly manifest the abundance of money, love, relationships, health, and happiness you've always wanted?

It is conceivable to believe that the Law of Attraction is a universal principle. Many have heard about the principle, some believe it isn't real, and some aren't even aware of it. However, if you came to realize that the Law of Attraction is true and you could fulfill any wish you've ever had, would you? This boundless power is accessible to everyone, yet only a small percentage of us are really employing it because they don't understand it, but that is about to change.

You may be familiar with the concept of manifestation or the Law of Attraction. But before we get to that, it is important to remember that while manifesting is about making your dreams come true, it doesn't mean it will happen when you sleep or in the middle of the night. You have to work towards achieving what you want and stay committed to it. Staying committed and working towards something is a tiny sum to pay (in my humble opinion) for something that can have such a tremendous impact on your life.

Since Albert Einstein's $E = MC^2$ equation was published, the world has discovered that all of life is energy. Everything is made of energy, as science teaches us. It is contained within the fundamental unit of matter. The same energy that makes up your body also makes up the bricks that make up your home. Your car, phone, animals, and trees - everything is made up of energy. Essentially, this indicates that all life, including you and me, is made up of energy.

Scientists tell us that the Universe is constantly expanding at an accelerating rate; humans are a part of creation (i.e., the Universe), a manifestation of the dynamic, creative, and incredible power of the Universe to create life and expand on its own, both in time and space. This is because just as the Universe continues to expand, humanity grows and evolves. The Law of Attraction is the magnetic property that allows for this type of creation and expansion of the Universe to take place. For us humans, this means that the Law of Attraction is responding to the thoughts, words, feelings, and actions that we have and express.

The following is the foundation of the work we'll be doing:

- The Universe is made up of energy.

- Every molecule of matter vibrates at a certain frequency. This implies that the things you want and don't want are both vibrating at a certain frequency.

- Vibration draws vibration, and the two are inseparable.

According to quantum physics, everything vibrates; everything is energy, and our thoughts are cosmic waves brimming with strong energy. It appears that we are all made up of energy, that we are all part of a "sea" of energy. This means our thoughts are important because we are part of universal consciousness. As we move through the Universe, our thoughts and feelings send forth cosmic waves, which contribute to shaping it. The concept of the Law of Attraction reflects that we attract what we put out, vibrations attract similar vibrations - like attracts like.

You can't deceive the Universe; it will match the vibration you emit. For example, when you are vibrating at a high frequency, amazing things flow naturally to you, and you constantly run into the best people and circumstances (and vice versa). When you consciously control your energy, trust in the unseen, and maintain your greatest frequency, you activate your intrinsic ability to create the reality you wish. To improve your vibration, you must believe that you can have everything you want. And the most effective approach to sustain this belief is to maintain a connection to Source Energy.

Mood Tracker

Your mood impacts your thoughts, feelings, and actions. There are 30 polaroids in the section below; you are to paint in the color that best describes your mood for that day. Four colors represent four moods. Yellow represents "Great," Baby Pink represents "Good," Blue represents "Average," and Red represents "Bad." For example, if you are feeling great, you color the polaroid for that day Yellow. If you are feeling sad that day, color the polaroid Red.

This should be done over the course of a 30-day period, meaning one polaroid per day. This mood tracker will provide you with a clearer view of your mood over time, so become aware of the areas you need to work on. If you have too many red days, you will become aware that you need to work on the factors causing that mood.

Mood Tracker

□ Great □ Good □ Average □ Bad

Mood Tracker

☐ Great ☐ Good ☐ Average ☐ Bad

Mood Tracker

☐ Great ☐ Good ☐ Average ☐ Bad

Key Concepts Underlying Manifesting

Let's look at some of the key concepts underlying manifesting and why it works:

Rule 1: Your inner world determines what reality you attract. Whether you know it or not, you manifest all the time. This means that the status of your inner world continues to attract people, events, and results.

Your inner world consists of your emotions about yourself and the world, your thought patterns, and your assumptions about what you can and cannot achieve. The outside world includes everything outside of oneself, such as your connections, income, and so on.

Your inner world has a big impact on what you create or attract in the outside world. So, depending on your ideas, beliefs, and emotions about yourself and the Universe, you may end up restricting yourself and attracting unwanted things (like lack), or you can materialize anything you genuinely desire.

Yes, the Law of Attraction will send opportunities and circumstances your way, and the world will conspire to help you realize your wishes. When it comes to manifesting, many people often approach it from the perspective of "How can I make myself feel better?"

However, it is better to ask, "How can I feel better so that I can attract more greatness into my life?" rather than, "How can I get more greatness into my life?" The focus should not be on acquiring a new house or a new wardrobe, but on improving the internal condition.

Rule 2: What you attract in the outside world changes as you alter your inner world.

It is possible to alter your inner world, including your convictions and views about what is feasible for you, as well as how you feel about yourself. These changes in your inner world will then appear in your outside world - what you attract into your life through the principles of the Law of Attraction.

One common fallacy regarding the Law of Attraction is that all you have to do is think about what you want a lot, and it will appear in your life. There is more to the Law of Attraction than just wishing for things. It's about how we feel, think, and believe. Our energy is made up of these things. The term "vibration" can also be used to describe this. When we think or feel things that match what we already believe, we will bring them into our lives. We will also bring things into our lives that make us feel the same way. You have to be a good match for what you want. This means that your thoughts, feelings, and beliefs must all be in line with what you want. Changing your beliefs is a vital aspect of the manifesting process, but it is just the beginning.

The second section is about your emotions. We're continually manifesting. Your thoughts shape your energy, and your experiences are the manifestations of your energy. It's all about what you think and how you feel. We send out a burst of energy that radiates from our bodies as we think. The likeness of this energy is drawn to it. In other words, if you're constantly thinking, "I'm a loser," you'll attract/manifest experiences into your life that affirm that belief.

"Every time you subtract negative from your life, you make room for more positive."

Unknown

When you think positive thoughts, you manifest positive experiences into your life. By thinking and feeling, "I'm awesome," you attract positive experiences into your life. Our physical bodies are constantly being energized by the energy we generate with every thought we have.

If you think about visualizing more money but don't believe you deserve it, your thoughts and feelings are at odds. These sentiments (inner world) will therefore be present in your manifested reality. Your sentiments and ideas about what you want should be in sync and as free of mental and emotional blockages as possible for a speedy and effective manifestation.

To manifest things, it is not only the thought process that is crucial; your goals, mission, or vision are just as important as your thought process. Every human being has a distinct and ever-changing set of priorities or a value hierarchy. Whatever is at the top of that list – your most important value – will serve as the foundation for and drive your purpose or mission.

Moving into Alignment and Staying There

Anyone who wants something must be in sync with it. To have what you're in harmony with is the only way to get what you're after. Alignment is a common word in the language of the Law of Attraction. It means that you are in sync with what you want. When you get what you want, you feel good about it, you're relaxed and happy, and there's just that sense that it's going to happen. On the other hand, attempting to attain any goal or desire while your energy is misaligned is akin to running while carrying a 90-pound weight. The appearance of unpleasant thoughts and uncomfortable feelings is a sign that your energy is split. A part of you desires something, while another part doubts your capacity to get it. Split energy not only feels bad, but it also prevents us from receiving our desires.

Alignment is our true natural state; It's a non-resistance state. It is the state where we easily allow our desires to manifest. For example, if you want to have more riches and abundance in your life, you must first feel richness and abundance.

Here are three effective strategies for harmonizing your energy to attract your desires more easily:

#1 Identify your secret allegiances.

Every minute and with every thought and feeling we express, we give life to one of two realities: a reality we do not choose to live or a reality we do. Many of us are linked unconsciously with the very realities we strive to avoid creating. We create these realities by contemplating them and thereby feeding them with our energy. To connect your energy with any desired outcome, such as joy, love, or ease, you must first determine what you are aligned with. Paying attention to your daily thoughts and how they make you feel will disclose any secret allegiances.

#2 Re-align your energy to recognize your rightful position in the Universe

Perception and reality are linked. When we view ourselves as insignificant, weak, and at the mercy of forces greater than ourselves, this perception becomes our reality. However, when we alter our perspective, our entire life experience changes. Re-align your energy to recognize your rightful position in the Universe, the perfection of the Universe that you were born in; when you understand that you are a vital component of this energy stream, practicing alignment becomes much easier.

#3 Align your energy with the presence, not the lack, of your desire.

What you concentrate on manifests in your life. Through the power of concentration, you conjure potent creative energy. And this energy is the foundation of every manifestation. To attract greater ease, success, love, or laughter, you must connect your energy with their presence. Recognize that they are immediately available to you, regardless of your current situation.

Instead of deferring your enjoyment to the future, pursue things that bring you happiness in the present. Permit yourself to feel fantastic for no reason. Permit yourself to relax, have fun, and appreciate the numerous benefits that surround you. You were born with the intrinsic ability to match your energy with the potent energy that produces and sustains the Universe. And while you do so, you receive a steady stream of thoughts and ideas. Like a cook in a well-stocked kitchen, you have everything necessary to build a joyful and fulfilling existence.

Goals

In this section, take the time to figure out what you desire. It may be something you already know, or it might be something you are still trying to figure out. There is no rush; you can decide to come back to complete this exercise when you feel confident in your choices.

This list should be hierarchical, i.e., writing down what you consider your most important goals first and your least important goals after.

Ask for what you want after you've set your intention — and write it down

This exercise is divided into two parts. The first column is where you write your goals, and the second column is where you best describe how you will feel when these goals become a reality.

Goals

Describe how the realization of this manifestation will make you feel

Goals

Describe how the realization of this manifestation will make you feel

Goals

Describe how the realization of this manifestation will make you feel

CHAPTER THREE

The Manifestation Method

"Visualization is daydreaming with a purpose."
- Bo Bennett

Visualization will always play a crucial role in manifestation. Because we're dealing with energy, the subconscious mind doesn't know the difference between what's real and what's not. The initial step of the manifestation process is to imagine what it would be like to get everything you want. With your eyes closed, let images appear before your inner eye. Having visual signals and reminders of what you want in your living or workplace might help you develop ideas about your intended goal on a regular basis. Repetition is a useful technique for activating The Law of Attraction.

The manifestation process relies heavily on imagination since it offers your goal a framework. Allow yourself to enjoy the feeling of what it would be like to already have what you seek as you envision yourself getting it. Concentrate on how it feels to have a large sum of money in your bank account, what you'll do with it, and how you'll see and experience the world differently.

The key is to concentrate on and then retain the sensation you have while visualizing and envisioning what you want. The Law of Attraction is activated by this sensation (or, more precisely, the sensation's energy). Repeat this practice for at least 2-5 minutes each day, and observe how your desire manifests in unexpected ways. While practicing this, you can go through the list you created in the exercise of the previous chapter if you need a reminder, or you could update your list if you so desire.

Applying the Manifesting approach multiple times each day is beneficial. In truth, the Manifesting technique is difficult to "overdo." The more you do it, the more effectively and quickly you will attract what you want.

After a while, you'll notice that your want is becoming closer, more genuine, and "doable." This is a sign that it is about to happen. Being explicit about what you want to create or attract into your life can be quite beneficial.

"Dreaming about what you want" or "magnetizing your wish/dream" are terms used to describe the Manifesting approach. In the realm of energy, what you "dream about" in this manner becomes a "magnet" that attracts what you want.

> *"To bring anything into your life, imagine that it's already there."*
> *-Richard Bach*

Treasure mapping is a technique that has grown in popularity around the world as a way to assist individuals in manifesting their goals. A vision board, also known as a dream board, essentially involves cutting out photographs and inspirational statements from magazines or printing images that symbolize what you wish to accomplish in your life and arranging them beautifully on a poster board. When you're finished, hang the board in plain sight so you can feed your subconscious mind with the pictures and start using the Law of Attraction to your advantage.

The time and procedures you take to construct your treasure map may be quite helpful in getting the process started. Sorting through photographs forces you to define what you're looking for. You're going to experience a range of emotions as you sift through and classify the photographs you desire for your treasure map. Perhaps you'll be enthralled and inspired. More significantly, you may quickly realize that you have anxieties and emotions about bringing the item you desire into your sphere of expertise. That's quite helpful! Take note of what emotions you experience during this process. Listen to what your inner voice has to say about your abilities to achieve your goals. What are your thoughts about your worthiness or abilities, or better yet, what are they saying about you?

This second step of the manifesting process, which is often overlooked but is a crucial step in fully accessing the Law of Attraction, is action. We previously "aligned" the mental (imagining/visualization) and emotional (feelings) towards the desired goal.

It is now time to perform "aligned" action. Through this, your whole being will be in perfect equilibrium on all levels: physical, emotional, and mental. This alignment assures that you will materialize your desires through the Law of Attraction.

The difficulty is to have both components - energy and action - working in unison. Until your energy is correctly aligned with what you really want, every action you perform will need far more effort to accomplish your desire, if it accomplishes anything at all.

There are two components to "aligned" action.

#1   Manifesting by acting "AS IF." Behaving AS IF is the most effective strategy to overcome our ingrained self-limitations. These self-limiting practices are diametrically opposed to the manifestation of what you want. To get aligned, conduct yourself AS IF. Even if you've never heard of acting "as if," you've probably heard of its relative – "fake it 'til you make it." The primary purpose of acting as if is to act "as if" a dream has already been realized, rather than chasing it. You learn to be the thing in your life that you desire. And when you do, you will unleash the true power of manifestation and the law of attraction to assist you in achieving your goals.

#2   "Doing everything it takes to get your desire one step closer."

The second component of taking "aligned" action is rather straightforward - you just need to identify what action moves you closer to the desired manifestation. For instance, to attract a better and healthier relationship, begin by being more receptive to others. This may involve talking to more people or initiating discussions when you normally would not. Typically, this entails venturing outside your comfort zone.

The critical point is to demonstrate to the "Spirit" that you are serious about your aim and that you really want to change and become, for example, a person who has a relationship. Again, the same holds true for anything you want to attract - success, wealth, wonderful companions, and so forth.

Four Principles of Attracting What You Want

Purify your Mind: Before you begin the manifestation process, it is necessary to purify your mind of any negative thoughts or doubts that may have crept into your consciousness. Begin a daily prayer practice in which you beg the Universe to release you from any self-limiting ideas that prevent you from realizing your full potential.

Get clear: When it comes to manifesting your desires, clarity is essential. Concentrate on, and be explicit about, your goals. Describe the attributes as though your manifestation was built only for you. Discuss your aspirations in the present tense, as if they have already occurred. Note all the elements about the work that make you happy, such as the office, the people, the money, how it makes you feel, and so on, if you're becoming clear about the job you desire.

Consider, feel, and believe it! Take your clear objective and spend time each day sitting in the sensation of achieving it. Meditation and visualization techniques might help you relish the experience. Allow the idea to guide the emotion and the feeling to inspire your energy.

Relax and unwind! Believe that the Universe has a better plan than you. Even if you know what you desire, you have no control over when or how it will arrive. Keep your cool, relax, and believe that the Universe is on your side! Keep your eyes, thoughts, and heart open to what the Universe has in store for you. Concentrate on being grateful for what you have now and for what you will get in the future.

Manifestation Photo board

The use of creative imagination combined with emotion has a major influence on your ability to attract something into your life. Print the photos that capture what you desire and paste them in the area below.

MANIFESTATION VISION BOARD

MANIFESTATION VISION BOARD

MANIFESTATION VISION BOARD

MANIFESTATION VISION BOARD

CHAPTER FOUR

Struggle vs. Strength

"It is not the strength of the body that counts but the strength of the spirit."
- J. R. R. Tolkien

Once upon a time, Frederick Douglas said, "Without a struggle, there can be no progress." Nobody enjoys struggle. Struggles are distressing, exhausting, humiliating, compromising, and painful. However, struggles are an unavoidable part of existence. They are intended to build you up rather than tear you down. What matters is how you react to such situations. Do you sit back and let yourself be overrun by struggles, or do you stand tall and decide to fight back? Some people don't realize that the battle is only a steppingstone on the journey to being who you were intended to be.

Like Joseph Campbell said, "It is by going down into the abyss that we recover the treasures of life. Where you stumble, there lies your treasure." We may unleash the riches inside by exploring the depths of our subconscious minds. We may silence the noise of competing voices and free up our potential to attract what we desire by looking at our limiting beliefs, negative thinking patterns, and conditioned reactions from years of learning and habit. You may silence those out-of-tune voices that contradict your intended result, silence those that undermine your vision and set the framework to increase your efficacy with the Law of Attraction.

"I'm convinced that we Black women possess a special indestructible strength that allows us to not only get down, but to get up, to get through, and to get over."
- Janet Jackson

Those are powerful words by Janet Jackson. Nonetheless, that statement doesn't mean that black women were built to struggle because of the strength they possess. No, it reflects the strength in our vulnerability. Nothing, in my opinion, strengthens you more than vulnerability and the ability to express your emotions.

In this life, there is pain and struggle. If you take the time to pay attention to your own thoughts, you'll notice that they're always at odds with reality. To have or not have anything is a matter of preference. The accomplishments and grass will always seem grander and greener on the other side.

You may find yourself struggling, not getting the results you want, having a hard time at work, or feeling out of place, like you don't belong; to put it another way, we are perpetually miserable and "suffering/struggling" because we desire things to be different from how they currently are. No matter how hard we try, we can never attain serenity or contentment in the present moment.

Even if we don't want it, most of what we attract in our life is the product of the thoughts and feelings we've had in the past. Unwanted experiences are attracted to and evoked by persistent negative beliefs. So, a positive outlook is a powerful and essential technique to establish the groundwork for success. To fight against struggles and to turn your struggles into a positive outcome, you have to be willing to transform your life. That is the foundation of the Law of Attraction. To ensure that your future is filled with pleasant experiences, it's important to be aware when your thoughts veer off course, and correct them.

However, don't beat yourself up if you make mistakes, struggle with things, or feel pessimistic. That only serves to increase your sense of self-doubt, which is ultimately counterproductive and will leave you struggling even more. Do your best to maintain an optimistic outlook, and then continue reading to learn more about how to turn things around.

Highlights of the Day

"In a world filled with distraction, attention is our competitive advantage."
- Jocelyn K. Glei

In the section below, I want you to write out the highlight of each day. It has 30 lines that represent every day of a month; for example, on the first day, the highlight for that day may be that you got to spend time with your family and friends.

This helps you appreciate the moments that you may otherwise have not paid attention to. Practicing gratitude is a great practice that will help in the actualization of your desires.

Highlight

of the day

1. _____

2. _____

3. _____

4. _____

5. _____

6. _____

7. _____

8. _____

9. _____

10. _____

11. _____

12. _____

13. _____

14. _____

15. _____

16. _____

17. _____

18. _____

19. _____

20. _____

21. _____

22. _____

23. _____

24. _____

25. _____

26. _____

27. _____

28. _____

29. _____

30. _____

31. _____

Create the Life of Your Dreams

The art of writing has a greater impact than most people realize. In this section below, I want you to create the life of your dreams. What do you desire most? How do you wish your life to turn out?

Ask yourself these questions as you create the life of your dreams. Write as though everything you have ever dreamed of has come to pass. For example, if you desire to get the position as the CEO of a firm, you could write, "I am overjoyed and grateful that I am the CEO of a major firm. My life is fantastic, and all the staff under me respect and trust my capabilities as their leader...."

Use the space provided below to create the life of your dreams!

Date: _____

I am overjoyed and grateful now that...

_____

_____

_____

_____

_____

_____

_____

_____

_____

_____

_____

_____

_____

_____

_____

_____

_____

_____

_____

_____

_____

_____

_____

Date: _____

I am overjoyed and grateful now that...

_____

_____

_____

_____

_____

_____

_____

_____

_____

_____

_____

_____

_____

_____

_____

_____

_____

_____

_____

_____

_____

_____

_____

_____

_____

Date: _____

I am overjoyed and grateful now that...

_____
_____
_____
_____
_____
_____
_____
_____
_____
_____
_____
_____
_____
_____
_____
_____
_____
_____
_____
_____
_____
_____
_____
_____
_____
_____
_____

Date: _____

I am overjoyed and grateful now that...

_____

_____

_____

_____

_____

_____

_____

_____

_____

_____

_____

_____

_____

_____

_____

_____

_____

_____

_____

_____

_____

_____

_____

_____

_____

Date: _____

I am overjoyed and grateful now that...

_____

_____

_____

_____

_____

_____

_____

_____

_____

_____

_____

_____

_____

_____

_____

_____

_____

_____

_____

_____

_____

_____

_____

Date: _____

I am overjoyed and grateful now that...

_____

_____

_____

_____

_____

_____

_____

_____

_____

_____

_____

_____

_____

_____

_____

_____

_____

_____

_____

_____

_____

_____

_____

_____

_____

Date: _____

I am overjoyed and grateful now that...

_____
_____
_____
_____
_____
_____
_____
_____
_____
_____
_____
_____
_____
_____
_____
_____
_____
_____
_____
_____
_____
_____
_____
_____

CHAPTER FIVE

Self-Love - Perfectly Imperfect

"Self-love, self-respect, self-worth: There's a reason they all start with 'self.' You can't find them in anyone else."

- Unknown

Self-Love Test

Do you mistake Self Reliance for Self-Love?

Are you in love with yourself? Do you show yourself love?

Even if you believe you do, the reality may surprise you. When was the last time you complimented yourself?

To determine your starting point, take the test on the following page. The result will give you a good idea of what you need to work on to improve your self-esteem.

We practice self-love so that we can overcome our limiting beliefs and live a life that truly shines.

Take the test again after a few weeks to see how far you've come.

"In order to love who you are, you cannot hate the experiences that shaped you."

Andrea Dykstra

Test Questions

1. What exactly does self-love entail for you?

2. What aspects of your personality do you already enjoy?

3. How do you feel about yourself right now?

4. What are your beliefs about loving and accepting oneself?

5. Can you identify any restrictions or conditions that you can let go of in order to love yourself even more?

6. How do you love those closest to you?

7. What do you require to be more at ease with your own being?

8. Who or what are you holding on to that is no longer beneficial to your well-being?

9. What do you consider to be your most valuable asset?

10. What does it take to make you happy?

11. What can you do to modify the way you're feeling in the moment?

12. What do you do to feel better when you're not feeling well?

13. What is something you've always wanted to try but haven't gotten around to it?

14. In what way could you possibly love yourself enough to... forgive yourself, nourish yourself, move your body, feed your soul, and live in the present moment?

Answers

1._____

_____

_____

2._____

_____

_____

3._____

_____

_____

4._____

_____

_____

5.

6.

7.

8.

9.

10.

11.

12.

13.

14.

"Love yourself enough to set boundaries. Your time and energy are precious. You get to choose how you use it. You teach people how to treat you by deciding what you will and won't accept."
- Anna Taylor

Love is a universal emotion that we often save for people who are closest to us. The fortunate recipients of our love are those dear people who have found their way into our hearts. However, before we can demonstrate genuine affection for others, we must first begin with ourselves. While self-love is the purest and most essential type of love, it is not often the most straightforward to express.

We look for affection outside of ourselves since that is how we found love and stability as children. It was given to us as a reward for excellent behavior. But we didn't grow out of it; we continue to seek affection from others, despite the fact that the love you seek can only come from within. That is why someone else's affection will never make you completely happy, and you will never feel safe unless you are confident in your own talents.

But how can you boost your self-esteem and affection for yourself?

In the self-love movement, many of us have clung to the belief that to be loved, we must first love ourselves completely. Some people feel we need to have done everything we can to improve ourselves before we engage in a relationship or before we can be truly lovable in the eyes of another person. Being in a relationship does not necessitate or reflect our ability to be loved, nor does it necessitate or reflect our ability to love others.

Some people believe it's impossible to learn how to love ourselves on our own because we don't exist on our own. They believe that our ability to love ourselves typically depends on the amount of love we've experienced from others. Oftentimes, those who have struggled, who have had many disappointing relationships, long periods of loneliness, abusive relationships, or emotionally neglectful parents, think this way. This mentality can leave them feeling like they're failing or that there is something wrong with them. Nothing is wrong with you. You have just been going about it wrong.

One thing you are yet to realize is that self-love doesn't have to come from the love others choose to show you or not. I will admit that the love others shower on you can contribute to your journey to self-love, but it becomes wrong when you rely on them to determine how to love yourself. Consider self-love as a process, not an endpoint, and define it for yourself. There is no finish line at which self-love becomes complete. Self-love is neither constant nor permanent.

Another thing people sometimes confuse self-love for is self-reliance and perfection. Many people believe that perfectionism is a positive trait. However, you will see that such a mindset can have a detrimental impact when you begin to believe that self-love and happiness are something you must earn rather than being something you are entitled to. When we learn that perfection is not the prerequisite to being loved by other people or loving oneself, we may begin to practice self-acceptance and, maybe ultimately, self-love. You need to understand that the recognition and acceptance of your imperfection will help you through your journey to self-love.

Take a minute to pause the never-ending pursuit and simply gaze into yourself. Consider where you've come from and the beauty of the fact that you are alive. True happiness and love are found in appreciating what you have and experiencing what you have. At the end of your life, you want someone to tell tales of how wonderful your life was, how you accomplished all you ever desired!

Another technique that helps build self-love and acceptance is self-forgiveness. Again, self-forgiveness is often easier in principle than in reality, but one approach to letting yourself find forgiveness is to recognize the insight you acquired from a depressing experience. If a relationship doesn't work out, for instance, try not to be too hard on yourself for the months/years you spent in the other person's life or the behavior that you regret. Instead, you should consider what you've learned during those months that will be useful in the future. Self-love does not imply that we will never make errors; rather, it encourages us to accept responsibility when we do something we regret so that we can move on.

What is Self-love?

Self-Consciousness and Self-Knowledge

When you know yourself, you can be comfortable in your own skin, be loyal to yourself, and live in accordance with what is most important to you.

Being Proud of Who You Are

When you have self-love, you are proud of who you are, and it can help you become a better version of yourself. Self-love can help you build the confidence you need in life.

Self-Compassion And Self-Forgiveness Are Essential.

Realizing that we all make errors is a component of self-love; therefore, instead of berating yourself for past slip-ups or poor choices, forgive yourself and move on.

Recognizing That You Are Extraordinary As You Are.

Self-love is recognizing that you are an exceptional, one-of-a-kind individual while striving for self-improvement.

Assurance Of Self-Care

This is true even if others depend on you — you can't pour from an empty cup. Self-love involves your understanding that to be your best, you must prioritize your health and welfare.

Being One's Biggest Cheerleader

Self-love is providing yourself with the motivation you require to overcome obstacles, pursue your goals, and sometimes just get through the day.

Knowing That You Are Capable Of So Much Good Is Empowering.

Today, more than ever before, it is possible to accomplish remarkable kindness in life. The sense of self-love is energized by the realization of one's own strength.

Taking Ownership Of Yourself And Making The Most Of Your Life

Self-love means rising above unpleasant circumstances and adversity and doing the best you can despite them.

I've discovered that cultivating greater self-love in my life has increased my happiness levels, and I'm more cheerful and resilient when things go wrong in my life (which, let's face it, happens from time to time!). My confidence has grown, and I feel more at ease with myself and the world around me. In light of these considerations, self-love is unquestionably something worth cultivating, and I hope I have persuaded you to embark on your own self-love path! Self-love is this and much more. Choose self-love today!

"Self-love necessitates a never-ending quest of acting on your own behalf and caring for oneself, no matter how difficult it may be."

You are Perfectly Imperfect, Don't Let Anyone Tell You Otherwise

Humanity is difficult. Even if we arrived with a set of instructions, who in their right mind would read them? The only way to be "human" is to do so in our own unique way. Our flawed actions are an integral part of being human. We don't want to lose what makes us human, regardless of how frequently these "flaws" affect us.

"Flaws" are the vulnerabilities that reside on the periphery of our being with authenticity and rawness that can feel overwhelming at times. It's tempting to believe that we're the only ones who wade through the messiness of flaws, but we're not. We may do them with varying degrees of intensity, with varying consequences and levels of awareness, but we all have flaws. It is the exquisitely flawed art of being completely human.

"As hard as it is, owning who you are and knowing what you want is the only sure path to affirmation... I want women to know they can get out of any situation if they return to their core source of strength: themselves."
- Ashley Graham

CHAPTER SEVEN

Affirmations and How To Use Them Effectively

"Affirmations are our mental vitamins, providing the supplementary positive thoughts we need to balance the barrage of negative events and thoughts we experience daily."

- Tia Walker

Short, positive sentences you can affirmatively recite to yourself are called affirmations. We're in desperate need of positive thoughts and energies. Reciting positive affirmations at the start of the day or whenever you need a lift can help you see things from a new perspective. Incorporating positive affirmations into my morning ritual has been a game-changer for me. Affirmations have had a huge impact on my mental health, and they can help you too.

Affirmations can help you overcome low self-esteem and low self-worth. Whether you write down one or three affirmations a day for a month, you're likely to notice a significant shift in your mentality and self-esteem. To be honest, the actual glow-up isn't on the outside, but on the inside. When you learn to love and accept yourself as you are, you begin to glow from the inside out.

An affirmation is a self-help strategy used to boost self-confidence and belief in your own abilities. If you tell yourself things like, "I'm a good person," you're probably affirming yourself without even realizing it.

"The only thing I can offer is my best effort."

"I have what it takes to succeed."

"I'm confident in my abilities to succeed,"

These are some simple words of wisdom that can help you shift away from your perceived shortcomings and instead focus on your strengths — those you already possess and those you wish to cultivate.

Taking Action is Key

Repeating affirmations go a long way. Affirmations can help increase your motivation and confidence, but you must act. Consider affirmations as a step toward change rather than the change itself. For example, take that "friend" who is always inquiring about your personal life. You don't want to offend anyone, but you also don't want to answer their questions. When you start to feel your blood boil, an affirmation like "I can remain calm even when I am annoyed" may guide you to a habit of deep breathing or grounding exercises. These strategies, combined with your affirmations, will help you get through the stressful situation until you can politely flee. You were the one who brought about the change, not the affirmation. It did, however, provide a starting point.

Increasing their effectiveness

Affirmations are only one type of self-help tool. They, like other strategies, can provide some relief, but their effectiveness is usually dependent on how you use them. Making your own can help ensure that you select affirmations that will be most beneficial to you. Try the suggestions below to help you develop and use affirmations more effectively.

Place them in the present.

While affirmations may seem similar to goals, they do not function in the same way. Affirmations are used to help you change long-held patterns and beliefs. Acting as if you've already succeeded is a good way to effect change. A goal is still something you must work toward. Affirmations, on the other hand, boost your self-esteem by reminding you of what you can do right now.

Stock affirmations should be avoided.

These days, Affirmations can be found almost anywhere: T-shirts, inspirational images on social media, internet articles, and self-help blogs, to name a few. It's fine to use an affirmation that really stuck with you, but creating an affirmation tailored specifically to your goals works best. Affirmations can be about anything, so get creative and think about how you can make yours as specific as possible. Many people find it beneficial to connect affirmations to core values like kindness, honesty, or dedication. This can help you stay focused on what really matters to you.

Maintain your authenticity.

Affirmations are very effective when they focus on specific characteristics or realistic, achievable changes you want to make to those characteristics. Change is always possible, but some changes are easier to achieve than others. Affirmations cannot produce a change in every situation, and if your affirmation focuses on a statement that you do not believe in, it will have little effect.

1. Today, I've decided to be myself.

2. I am intelligent and capable.

3. I'm more than my circumstances.

4. I'm comfortable in my own skin.

5. I have the knowledge and skills to accomplish anything I set my mind to.

6. Regardless of the circumstances, I will use positive language and think positive thoughts.

7. I attract success.

8. Everything I desire is everything I am entitled to.

9. Today is going to be a productive day.

10. My black skin is radiantly lovely.

11. I will be the greatest version of myself.

12. I am abundant.

13. I manifest the wonderful day I desire.

14. I choose to accomplish great things.

15. My hair is beautiful and one-of-a-kind.

16. I make wise choices.

17. I am brimming with brilliant ideas.

18. I will complete all my objectives for the day.

19. I'm going to have a good day today.

20. I enjoy stepping outside my comfort zone to discover what the Universe has to offer.

21. My body has done and continues to do incredible things. It's stunning.

22. I intend to savor every second of every moment.

23. I will be the change I want to see in the world.

24. I am tenacious.

25. I pick my own path to happiness.

26. I am an amazing, beautiful black woman who deserves to be loved, respected, and treated with kindness.

27. I am open to any possibility that leads to a greater good.

28. I'm going to devote some time to myself.

29. I'm at ease saying "No" as a complete sentence.

30. Today, I'm going to make a positive change by doing something I've never done before.

31. In all my relationships, I will express gratitude.

32. I'm only thinking good things.

33. I was created by a higher power, and I am aware of who I am.

34. I attract joy and happiness into my life.

35. I am filled with self-assurance.

36. I will approach all challenges with gratitude, assurance, and zeal.

37. I'm not going to apologize for being myself.

38. I am confident in establishing and adhering to boundaries.

39. I respect everyone's path.

40. I am a kind and considerate friend.

41. Every experience has taught me something new.

42. I value all my relationships.

43. I'm open to new opportunities.

44. My success is under my control.

45. Today is a new day to start over.

46. I'm grateful for another day.

47. I am fit and strong.

48. My future is promising.

49. I have a lovely day ahead of me.

50. Every day, I am filled with positive energy and evolving with purpose.

51. I'm going to do something spectacular today.

52. I will not accept anything less than my absolute best from myself or others.

CHAPTER EIGHT

Emotional Visualization Scripts For Manifesting Love & Romance

---

"Your task is not to seek love, but merely to seek and find all the barriers within yourself that you have built against it."

Rumi

To attract your ideal soulmate, you should be clear about the critical characteristics you seek in someone, such as honesty, integrity, and dedication. It is critical to be specific about these characteristics since the Universal Law, or Law of Attraction, cannot respond to vacillating, half-hearted aspirations.

Additionally, you should compile a list of attributes that you are willing to offer your soul mate, such as good communication, comprehension, or whatever else is vital to you. Because relationships are two-way streets, you must be willing to offer the same attributes in return. Once you've compiled this list, you'll use it to develop an Intention Statement that will assist you in focusing on the loving conditions you seek, so allow enough time to brainstorm for significant words and ideas.

Creating an Intention Statement is one of the most powerful activities you can take as a co-creator with the Universe, as it clearly and precisely expresses what you want. Your Intention Statement does not need to be lengthy, but it must be clear about what you want. To include some of the phrases and concepts from your wish list into your statement, take a look at your list of ideal attributes. You can begin writing your Intention Statement with the words you've chosen once you've decided on the best ones.

In the following affirmations, pay attention to your feelings and use the ones that make you feel optimistic and hopeful when repeating them.

Love Affirmations

1.   I trust the Universe to send my true partner on time.

2. The Law of Attraction works the same for everyone.

3. I'm learning that changing my thinking can transform my life.

4. I'm using the Law of Attraction to attract my true mate.

5. I believe in my ability to produce real love.

6. I'm ready for a wonderful relationship.

7. My heart and life are open to a loving relationship.

8. I am open to receiving love.

9. I am proud of my ability to feel love and affection.

10. I am open to receiving the love energy that surrounds me.

11. I finally accept my rightful love and romance.

12. Every day I try to love more.

13. I chose to let love in.

14. I allow myself to enjoy love, romance, and a satisfying relationship.

15. I am ready to meet my soul mate.

16. I allow myself to fall madly in love.

Create a visualization script of your perfect date

Imagine going on the perfect date. Do you feel good? Do you feel happy? What would your ideal date entail? What qualities would you want him/her to possess? Create a visualization script of your perfect date below.

_____

_____

_____

_____

_____

_____

Create a visualization script of what it would be like to spend a romantic day with your soulmate

Imagine holding your soul mate's hand as you spend time together. How would it feel going down to the beach with your partner? Do you feel blessed to have a special someone in your life? Create a visualization script of what it would be like to spend a romantic day with your soulmate.

_____

_____

_____

_____

_____

_____

_____

_____

_____

_____

_____

_____

_____

_____

_____

_____

_____

_____

_____

_____

_____

_____

_____

_____

_____

Create a visualization script of what it would be like to spend the rest of your life with your soulmate.

Imagine all the sights, sensations, and feelings you'd have if you lived with your soul mate. Imagine waking up each day with someone precious at your side. How would eating with your soulmate feel? Create a visualization script of what it would be like to spend the rest of your life with your soulmate.

_____

_____

_____

_____

_____

_____

_____

_____

_____

_____

_____

_____

_____

_____

_____

_____

_____

_____

_____

_____

_____

_____

_____

_____

Manifesting Love Question And Answer Section

QUESTION: When can I expect to meet my true love?

ANSWER: How long it will take depends on if you're serious about manifesting your dreams. You need to put the time and effort into techniques like Intention Statement, Emotional Visualization, and verbal affirmations.

QUESTION: Which manifestation method is greatest for attracting romantic love?

ANSWER: You should use Emotional Visualization as much as possible if you are the type of person who is motivated by visuals and mental images. As an alternative, if you are more energized by the spoken word, you may choose to employ spoken affirmations to create good thoughts and expectations.

Question: What role will a Vision Board have in my search for love?

ANSWER: A Vision Board, also known as a Treasure Map or Goal Map, is an effective manifestation technique for attracting your soul match. You can create a Vision Board by gluing various items on a piece of card stock, such as words, photographs, or magazine cutouts. You must use images that make you feel optimistic and hopeful to help you create the things and conditions you seek. It's entirely up to you how big or little your Vision Board is.

Manifestation of Love and Romance Vision Board

Creative imagination combined with emotions can have a major influence on your ability to attract something into your life. Print the photos that capture what you desire in your love life, places you wish to visit with your partner, basically anything you want to do with your partner, and paste them on the area provided.

 # MANIFESTATION OF LOVE AND ROMANCE BOARD

MANIFESTATION OF LOVE AND ROMANCE BOARD

 # MANIFESTATION OF LOVE AND ROMANCE BOARD

# MANIFESTATION OF LOVE AND ROMANCE BOARD

CHAPTER TEN

Trust the Process

"Hold the Vision...drop the excuses...remember your why. Swerve around obstacles...trust the process. Happiness and success will find you."
- Karen Salmansohn

Manifestation is a collaborative effort. You choose what you want and place it in the Divine's hands. TRUST is a critical component that is frequently overlooked. If we follow the manifestation guidelines of having a burning desire backed by unshakable confidence, visualizing the outcome, and trusting until manifestation occurs, we can achieve our goals. The most important factor here is trust. You must have faith in the Universe to respond to your request.

Making sure you're in tune with universal energy and your life purpose is the first step toward trusting the Universe to deliver your manifestations. Next, keeping note of your manifestations is one of the most important things you can do to strengthen your faith and trust in the Universe! It's so easy to get caught up on what you want rather than thinking about or appreciating what you already have!

You must first realize that the life you are experiencing now is the life you created. Yes, the Law of Attraction is constantly in effect. Whether you like what you've manifested or not, you're always manifesting. For better or worse, the cosmos has granted your wishes and turned your ideas into reality.

As a result, acceptance is the first step toward trusting the cosmos. You acknowledge that you are already a master manifester! Accept that anything you have in your life is something you've already generated and brought into existence! This isn't to say you can't fix it.

Manifestation Tracker

Remember to always be grateful! Use the tracker below to track your Manifestation.

Trust the Process!

There are various exercises under this section. The first exercise is the "**Manifestation Inspiration**." This task has various categories, including Songs, Books, Videos, and Images. What you are required to do under this task is to fill in what inspires your manifestations in the text area provided under each category. For example, if a particular song inspires your manifestations in any way, write the name of the song in the text area provided under the "Songs" category, or if it is an image that inspires you, print it out and paste it on the "Photos" category. Keeping track of your inspirations can help you remember why you started the journey and keep you committed.

The second exercise is the **"Manifestation Log."** In this sheet, you will list out the exact things that you want to manifest under the left column, and right down how you will manifest it in the middle column. On the right column, write down exactly how you feel when you visualize yourself manifesting the desired result.

The third exercise is the "**Manifestation Affirmation Journal.**" Under this task, you journal your manifestation journey, or you can write specific affirmations that are important to your desires and how your manifestation journey is coming along.

The fourth exercise is "**Manifestation Habit Tracker.**" Under this task, you can track how well you practice various aspects of the manifestation process. This tracker was created to span a month. Every day of the month, when you practice any of the categories in this exercise, you can tick the box. There are five categories: Visualization, Affirmation, Gratitude, Meditation, and Scripting; whenever you practice any of these categories, ticking the box will help you keep track of your commitment.

The fifth exercise is **"Manifestation if it's coming."** You will work on your number 1 manifestation goal by writing down how you would feel when you manifest it, and exactly what you need to start and stop doing to achieve that. Think of the exercises and habits to implement in your life that will help you reach your manifestation goals faster, and the bad habits you may have that may be preventing you from reaching your goals.

The sixth exercise is the **"Manifestation Daily Planner."** where you can schedule your day, to-do lists, and acts as a journal with prompts and a place for self-reflection.

Manifestation inspiration

SONGS	BOOKS

IMAGES	VIDEOS

Manifestation inspiration

SONGS	BOOKS

IMAGES	VIDEOS

Manifestation inspiration

SONGS	BOOKS
IMAGES	VIDEOS

Manifestation Log

DESIRE	HOW DO I MANIFEST	HOW DO I FEEL

Manifestation Log

DESIRE	HOW DO I MANIFEST	HOW DO I FEE

Manifestation affirmation journal

DATE _____

Manifestation affirmation journal

DATE _____

Manifestation affirmation journal

DATE _____

Manifestation affirmation journal

DATE _____

Manifestation affirmation journal

DATE _____

Manifestation affirmation journal

DATE _____

Manifestation affirmation journal

DATE _____

Manifestation habit tracker

MANIFESTATION	AFFIRMATION	GRATITUDE	MEDITATION	SCRIPTIN.

Manifestation habit tracker

MANIFESTATION	AFFIRMATION	GRATITUDE	MEDITATION	SCRIPTING

Manifestation if it's coming

MY MANIFESTATION

WHAT WOULD I FEEL

WHAT WOULD I START DOING

WHAT WOULD I STOP DOING

Manifestation if it's coming

MY MANIFESTATION

WHAT WOULD I FEEL

WHAT WOULD I START DOING

WHAT WOULD I STOP DOING

Manifestation Daily Planner

THINGS THAT MADE ME SMILE TODAY	I AM GRATEFUL FOR
SCHEDULE	TO DO
	HEALTH AND WELLNESS, Actions to boost mental, spiritual and physical wellness
GOALS	GROWTH, "What i have learned"

NOTES

Manifestation Daily Planner

THINGS THAT MADE ME SMILE TODAY	I AM GRATEFUL FOR
SCHEDULE	TO DO
	HEALTH AND WELLNESS, Actions to boost mental, spiritual and physical wellness
GOALS	GROWTH, "What i have learned"

NOTES

Manifestation Daily Planner

THINGS THAT MADE ME SMILE TODAY	I AM GRATEFUL FOR
SCHEDULE	TO DO
	HEALTH AND WELLNESS, Actions to boost mental, spiritual and physical wellness
GOALS	GROWTH, "What i have learned"

NOTES

Manifestation Daily Planner

THINGS THAT MADE ME SMILE TODAY	I AM GRATEFUL FOR
SCHEDULE	TO DO
	HEALTH AND WELLNESS, Actions to boost mental, spiritual and physical wellness
GOALS	GROWTH, "What i have learned"

NOTES

Manifestation Daily Planner

THINGS THAT MADE ME SMILE TODAY	I AM GRATEFUL FOR
SCHEDULE	TO DO
	HEALTH AND WELLNESS, Actions to boost mental, spiritual and physical wellness
GOALS	GROWTH, "What i have learned"

NOTES

Manifestation Daily Planner

THINGS THAT MADE ME SMILE TODAY	I AM GRATEFUL FOR
SCHEDULE	TO DO
	HEALTH AND WELLNESS, Actions to boost mental, spiritual and physical wellness
GOALS	GROWTH, "What i have learned"

NOTES

Manifestation Daily Planner

THINGS THAT MADE ME SMILE TODAY	I AM GRATEFUL FOR
SCHEDULE	TO DO
	HEALTH AND WELLNESS, Actions to boost mental, spiritual and physical wellness
GOALS	GROWTH, "What i have learned"

NOTES

There is No Room For Excuses

One of the biggest hindrances to practicing manifestations is the excuses we make. In the end, it's excuses that keep us stuck. We create excuses to justify our inaction. The most important thing is to get started right away. I hope these quotes inspire you to stop making excuses and start living the life of your dreams.

"Maturity is when you stop complaining and making excuses in your life; you realize everything that happens in life is a result of the previous choice you've made and start making new choices to change your life."
- Roy T. Bennett

"You can have excuses, or you can have success; you can't have both."
- Jen Sincero

"When you are willing to replace mundane excuses with hard work and your laziness with determination, nothing can prevent you from succeeding."
- Prem Jagyasi

In the section below, there are two columns. Under the first column, "Your Excuses," write the excuses that are holding you back; the things you keep doing, saying, or thinking that are stopping you from manifesting your desires. Under the second column, write out what you can do to overcome the excuse you have been struggling with. At the end of this exercise, you will realize that a clearer view of the problem makes fixing it much easier.

Your Excuses	What actions will you take to get rid of it

Conclusion

"You become what you believe. And to believe that you are created by the power that's greater than yourself means anything is possible."
- Oprah Winfrey.

I want to sign off here by encouraging you to pursue your dreams and desire with the same belief that anything is possible as long as you manifest, take action, and trust the process. This journal will take you a long way. Journaling can assist you in clearing your mind and making critical connections between your thoughts, feelings, and behaviors.

In the various chapters of this book, I have carefully crafted it to serve as a guide to help you navigate your journey of manifestation - to first accept that you need to change things up, to believe that you are worthy, to act, to express gratitude, and to trust the process. There are various tasks in this book that require your participation and commitment. These tasks will help you understand the secrets of manifesting and how best to utilize it. Don't take it for granted. In the end, it will be worth it, I promise.

Believing that you can achieve anything you want in life - whether it's a great career, a great relationship, or a fantastic financial move - is the first step. And you are deserving of it. What's the harm in giving it a try? Allow yourself to be who you really are by providing yourself with the resources to do so. To deny yourself the life of your dreams out of fear of being criticized, rejected, or failure serves no one.

Manifesting is a lot simpler when you spend your time doing what makes you happy and what you're skilled at. You're cherished. There are wonders all around you. Believing that what you want is within your reach is the first step toward achieving it, and it is possible to have it all. Remember, regardless of the stakes; you must never give up hope. The Universe awaits you.

Thank You

"Happiness springs from doing good and helping others."
— Plato

Those who help others without any expectations in return experience more fulfillment, have higher levels of success, and live longer.

I want to create the opportunity for you to do this during this reading experience. For this, I have a very simple question... If it didn't cost you money, would you help someone you've never met before, even if you never got credit for it? If so, I want to ask for a favor on behalf of someone you do not know and likely never will. They are just like you and me, or perhaps how you were a few years ago...Less experienced, filled with the desire to help the world, seeking good information but not sure where to look...this is where you can help. The only way for us at Dreamlifepress to accomplish our mission of helping people on their spiritual growth journey is to first, reach them. And most people do judge a book by its reviews. So, if you have found this book helpful, would you please take a quick moment right now to leave an honest review of the book? It will cost you nothing and less than 60 seconds. Your review will help a stranger find this book and benefit from it.

One more person finds peace and happiness...one more person may find their passion in life...one more person experience a transformation that otherwise would never have happened...To make that come true, all you have to do is to leave a review. If you're on audible, click on the three dots in the top right of your screen, rate and review. If you're reading on a e-reader or kindle, just scroll to the bottom of the book, then swipe up and it will ask for a review. If this doesn't work, you can go to the book page on amazon or wherever store you purchased this from and leave a review from that page.

PS - If you feel good about helping an unknown person, you are my kind of people. I'm excited to continue helping you in your spiritual growth journey.

PPS - A little life hack - if you introduce something valuable to someone, they naturally associate that value to you. If you think this book can benefit anyone you know, send this book their way and build goodwill. From the bottom of my heart, thank you.

Your biggest fan **– Layla**

www.ingramcontent.com/pod-product-compliance
Lightning Source LLC
Chambersburg PA
CBHW081332120626
46546CB00011B/3312